OVA AVES

OVA AVES

Photographs by
Thaddeus Holownia
Poems by
Harry Thurston

ANCHORAGE PRESS

for Gay
& Cathy

Ultimately, there should be a language in which
the word 'egg' is reduced to O entirely.

—JOSEPH BRODSKY, *Ab Ovo*

THE COLOUR OF EGGS

> ... the motion of the egg affects the colour patterns. It is as if the innumerable brushes hold still while the canvas moves.
>
> —BERND HEINRICH

ALL BIRD EGGS have unique markings and colouration which are very much like a fingerprint. The colours of bird eggs are deposited by gland cells in the wall of the uterus. The pigments used in bird eggs are derived from waste blood and bile pigments. Gland cells secrete the background or 'ground colour' as well as the spots and/or streaks that occur (usually referred to as 'markings'). Spots occur if the egg remains stationary while the pigment is secreted; streaks and lines occur when the egg is turned during the application of pigment. Pigments function as camouflage as well as reducing the harmful radiation from ultra violet light. The eggs of ground and nesting birds are heavily pigmented while hole nesters are often completely white.

—GAY HANSEN

OVA AVES

We all must come from somewhere. Out of the blackness of time,
moon-faced, our complexions pocked by the catastrophe of beginnings.

Why not believe as did the ancient marsh dwellers?
The sacred ibis spoke the gods into being,

laying an egg from which the sun burst forth.
The rest is history. Or so said Herodotus.

It was the jet-black ibises, with their hooked beaks
down-turned like the nibs of pens, who gave us writing.

One story is as good as another.
We all must come from somewhere,

shining out of the blackness of time.
Believe what you must.

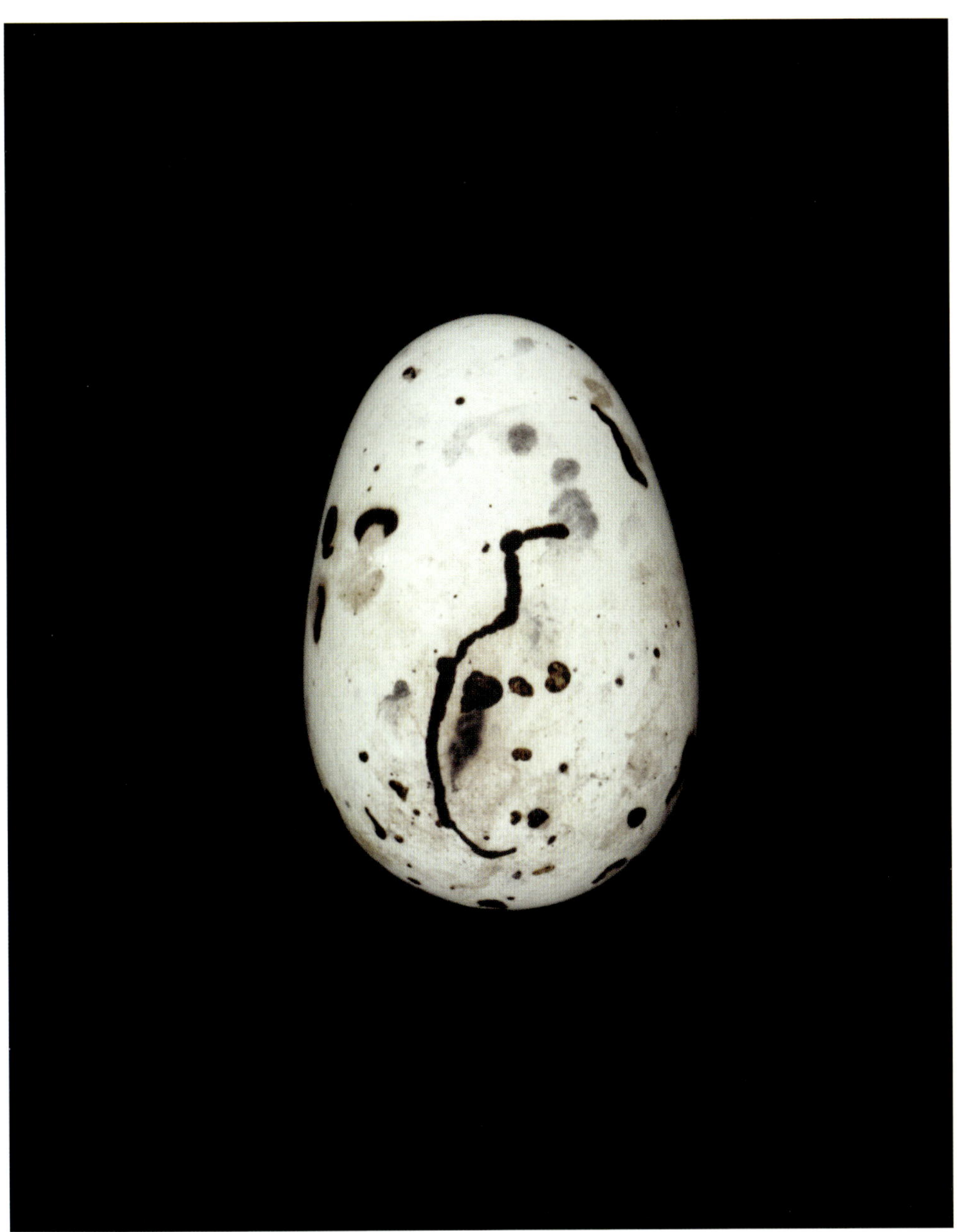

UNKNOWN

All bird guides begin with 'loon.'
You are most ancient, most prehistoric,

as all can attest who hear your call
oscillate across a dark lake, quirky as a quasar,

harking back to a time before humans
began to gawk at the night sky

(star-spangled like your back) and wonder,
whence all this cosmic commotion?

You are the spirit in the shaking tent,
the belief in an abiding mystery,

something alive in the mute cosmos
besides our nattering selves. A voice

that vibrates in the reptilian brain, echoing
an old word we once knew, need more than ever.

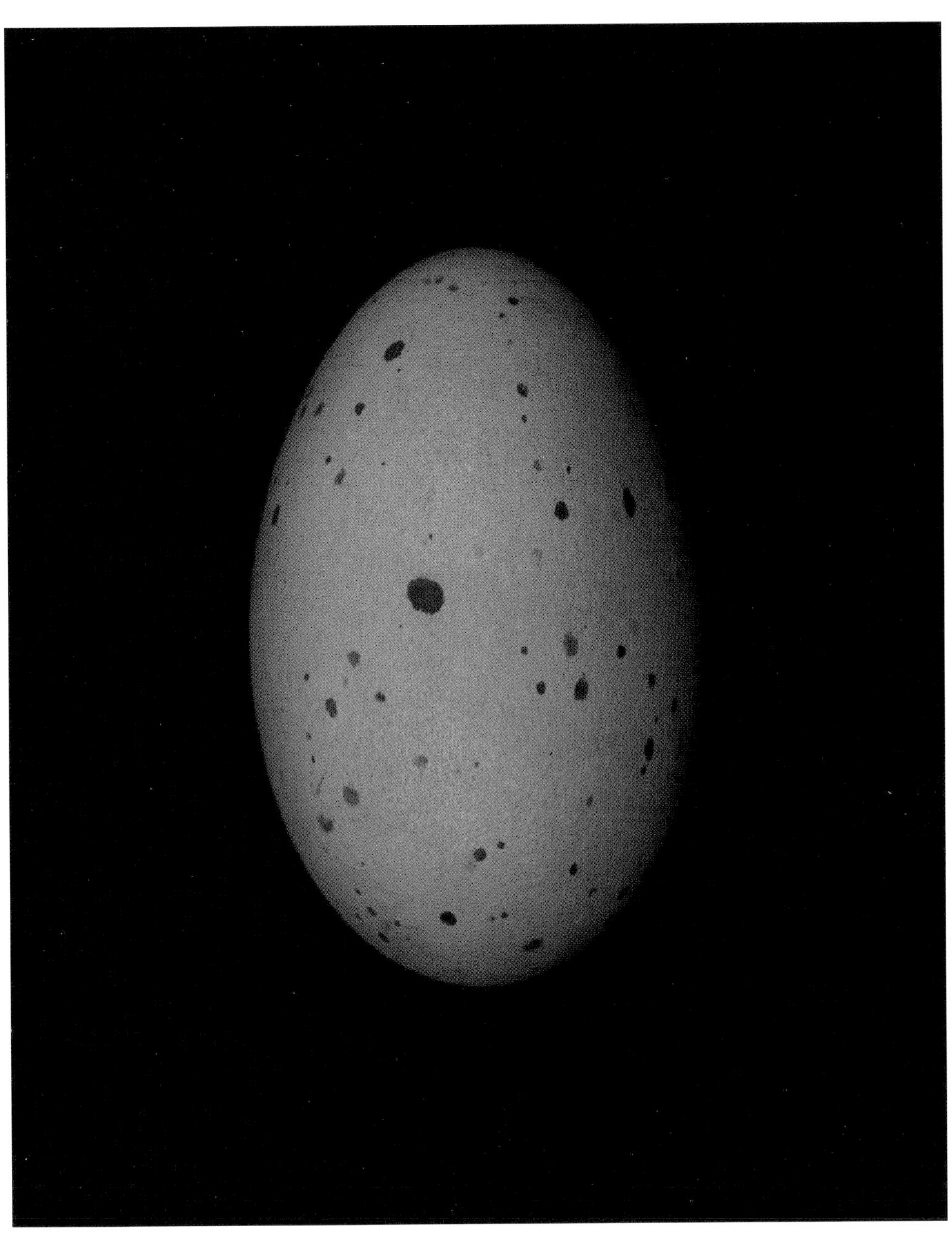

COMMON LOON

Gavia immer

A ghost is clasped within your inked cameo, the blue funk
of extinction, ancestral memory of all those who came ashore,

scurvy navvy and curator alike, club in hand,
to batter the Great Auk into oblivion.

Tuxedoed and noble, you preside at the continent's edge,
rejoicing at every empty wave.

The Atlantic roils below, while your egg, clever dervish,
twirls on its precarious ledge— without a great fall.

You gargle and mumble your complaint;
your guttural chorus erects a sentinel of sound,

to remind us of the cost of silence.

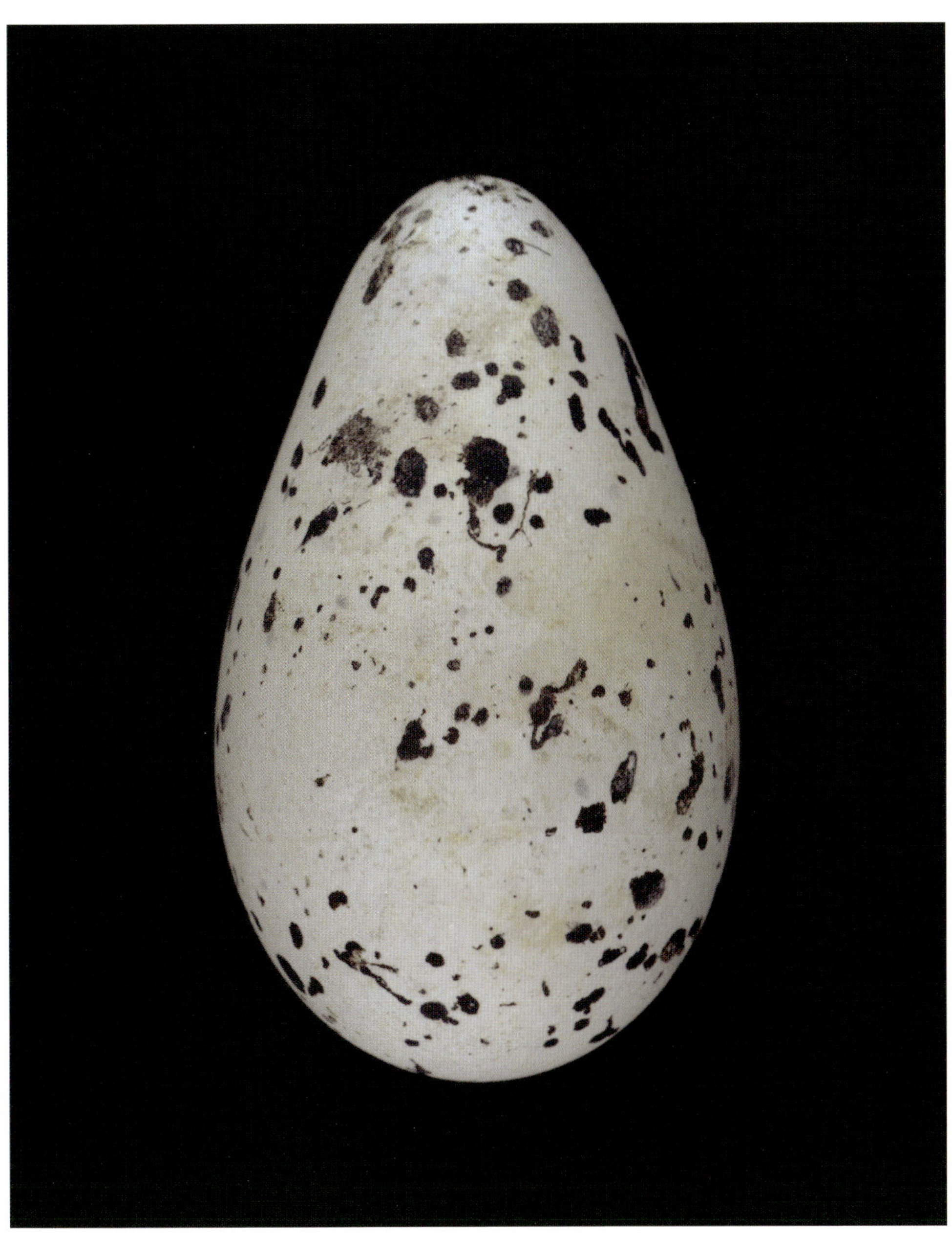

THICK-BILLED MURRE
Uria lomvia

'Land gull,' my friend says. Evolve backwards,
if you will, abandon the mothering sea,

follow in the chocolate wake of the plow,
forsaking the clean, blue line the keel makes.

Pick worms. Perhaps that is how you acquired
that indelible signature at the bill tip,

from too much probing in the black earth.
I am like that, too, carrying smudged words

at my fingertips. Loafing, waiting
for something to turn up, to swallow it whole.

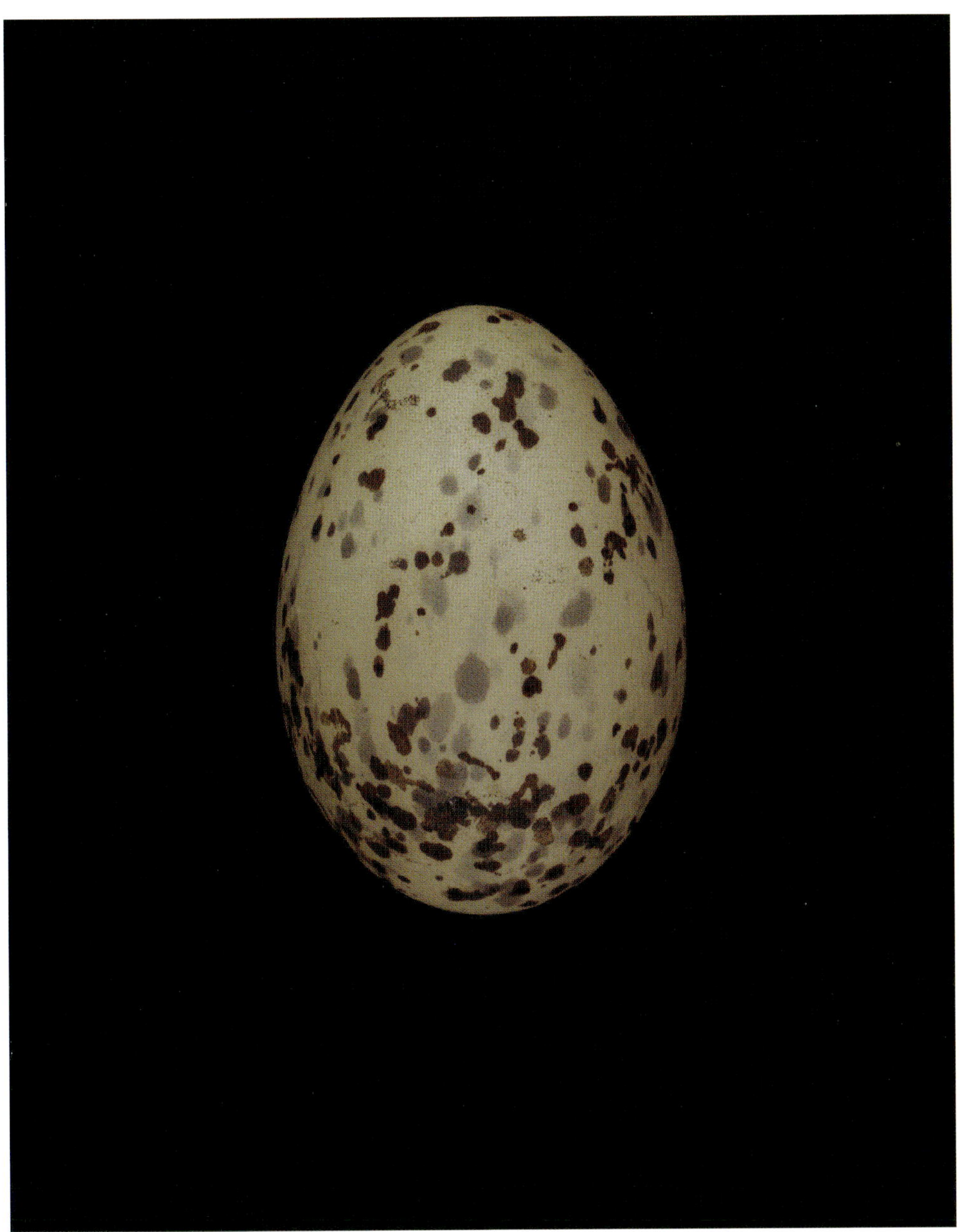

RING-BILLED GULL
Larus delawarensis

Parson, with your black vestments on your back,
ministering to the coming in, the going out,

I have seen you at work, lo, have walked
through your valley of birth and death.

When you turn your head, all heads turn
with one question in mind, an alarm,

'Why me, oh, why me!' When you toss
back your head as if to laugh,

it is the belly laugh of Saturn,
tearing asunder his own children.

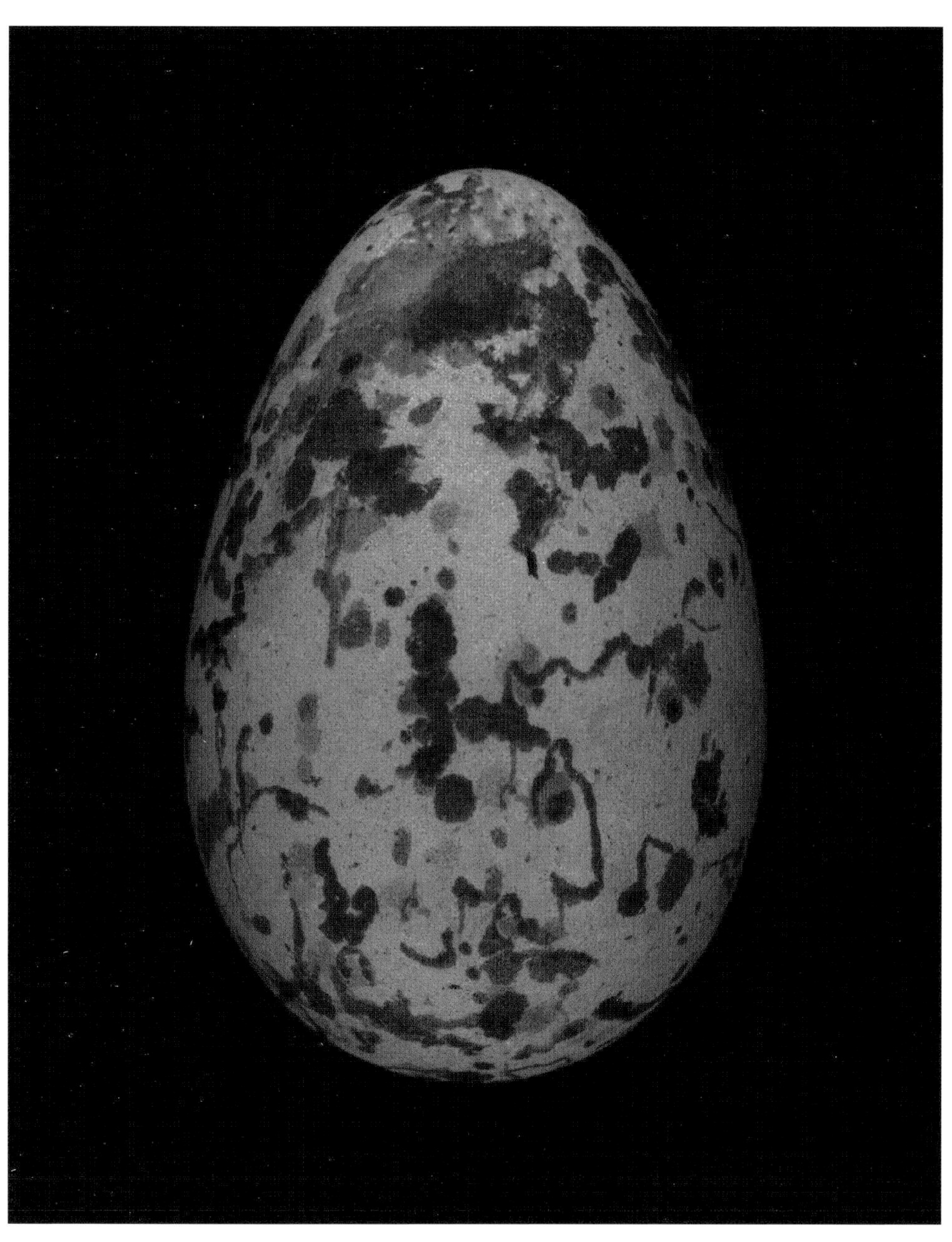

GREAT BLACK-BACKED GULL
Larus marinus

I saw one once, tracing an arctic circle, a rarity,
another entry for the list I do not keep.

Funny thing, its head was not black at all,
but brown, which is how you know it is not

Laughing, Sabine's, nor Bonaparte's, all black-headed.
Once I hurdled the literal, I liked the irony

of describing a thing for what it is not.
For once, science takes a flier.

Look, look there! 'What?' A black-headed gull!
'Where?' See! 'Which one?' The one with the brown cap.

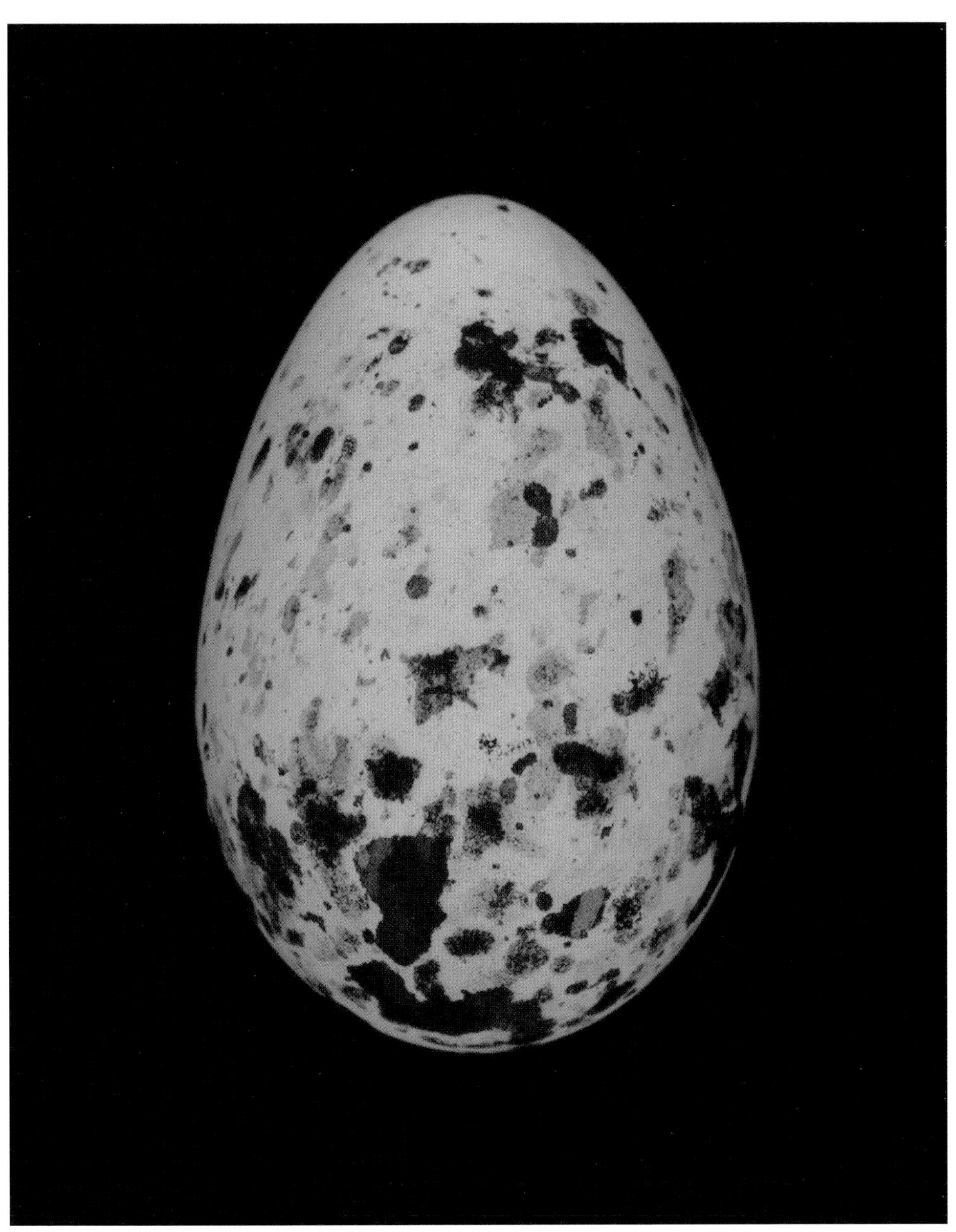

BLACK-HEADED GULL
Larus ridibundus

You might chide your mother for her seeming carelessness,
the shallow scrape where you lay. But who could gainsay her clever ploys?

She feigns this way and that, dragging her wing tip
in a sinuous line, hopscotching across the plain.

Thinking ourselves clever, we become fox,
taste the sweet flesh of this poor, earth-bound creature.

Following, we travel ever further from satisfaction.

Even you, dumb egg, play the decoy, lying
in the gravel, silent as any stone.

Soon, little one, you will put on your twin yoke
and meet the light, singing your mother's wiles.

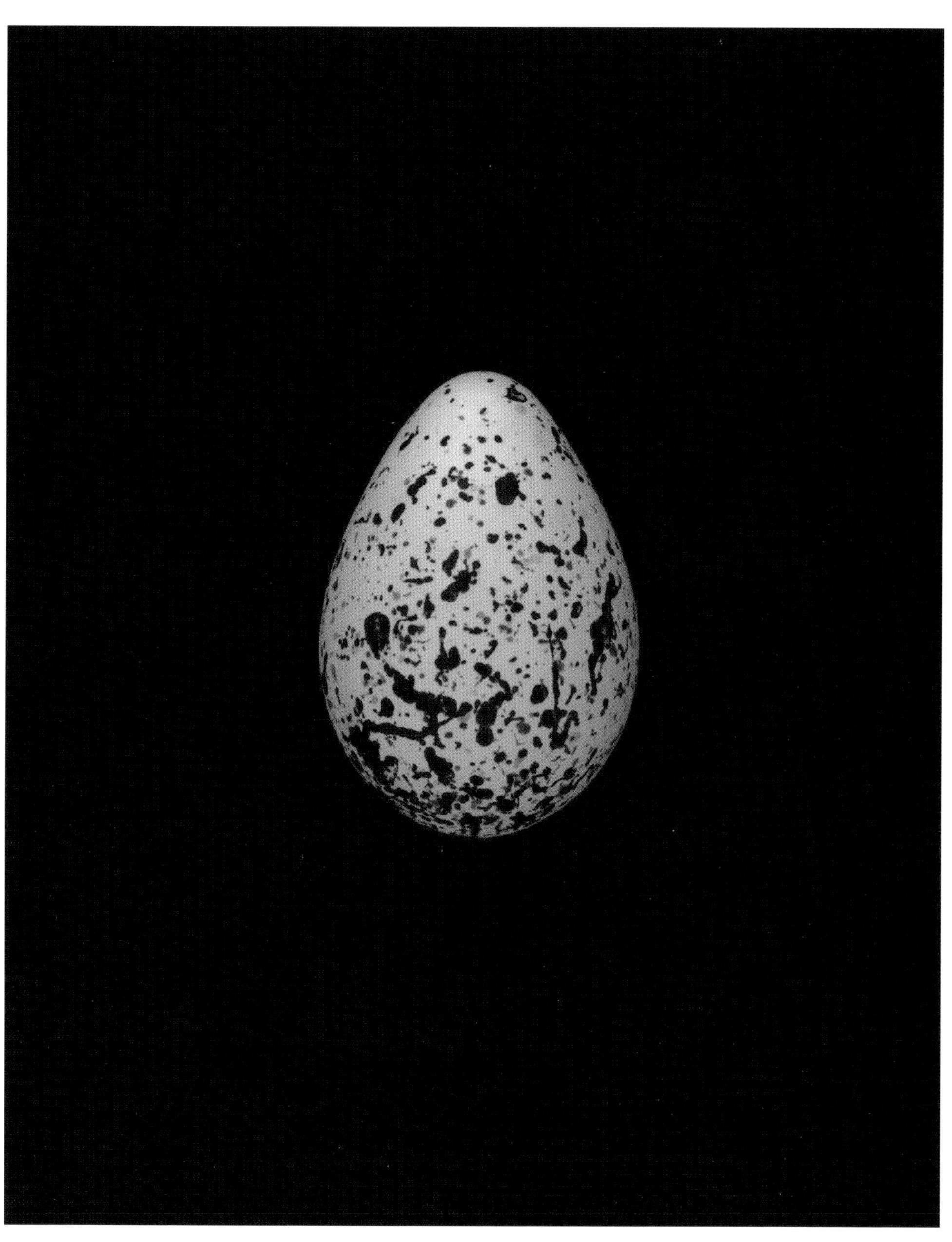

KILLDEER
Charadrius vociferus

White, nearly round as a cue ball, your egg might
roll true on that green tableland banked behind dykes—

Tantramar, maritime prairie the sea laid down,
grain by grain, when the tide was 'asking high.'

You tilt above this reclaimed place
like a bubble in a spirit level,

tipping by degrees, as if pondering
a question of loyalty, reparation for past injustice.

You yourself suspend the laws of nature,
hanging in the sky, stalled

on upswept wings,
calling all the shots.

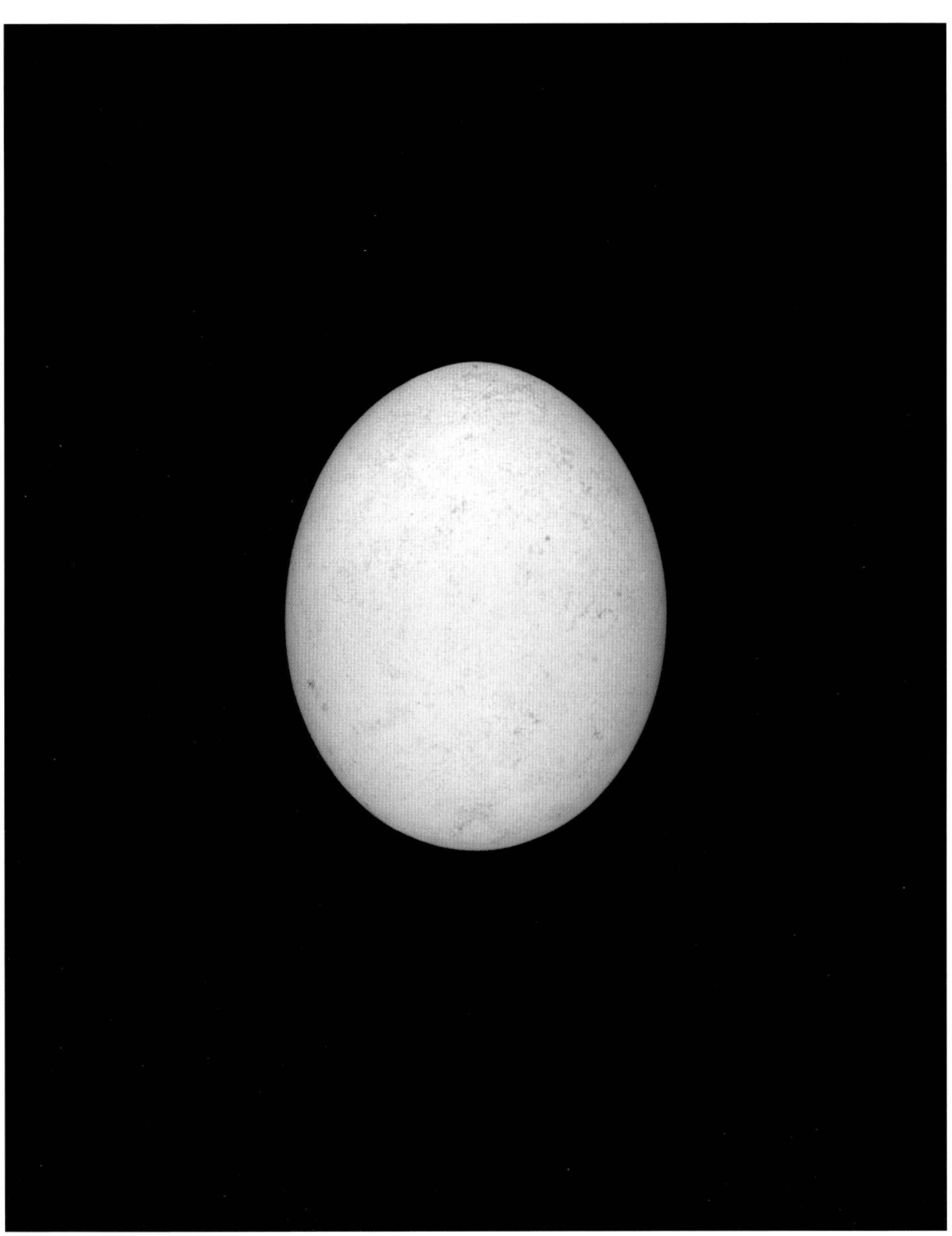

NORTHERN HARRIER

Circus cyaneus

All of us are worlds, planetary, alone,
wobbling through chaos.

From the egg of night was born Eros
who pierced us with life, even joy.

Burnt sienna and cobalt blue, the alchemy
of earth, sky and water, swirl in your hovering flight.

Stalled between ocean and heaven, when you drop,
stone-heavy, speed is your only mercy.

Held fast, the dead fly up to their gods,
bodies ablaze, molten with light.

Bone-breaker, you are the elevator of souls
who whistles while he works.

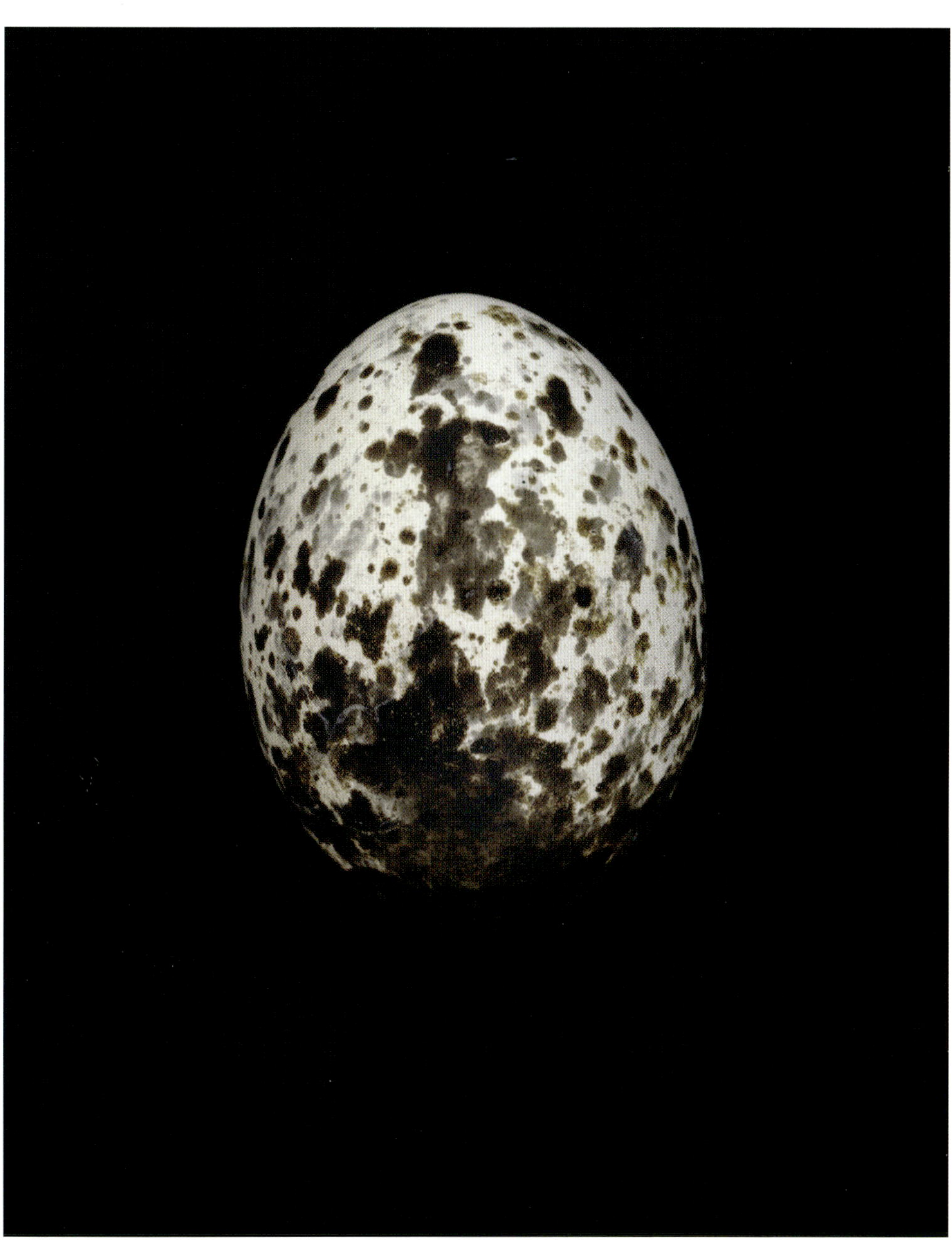

OSPREY
Pandion haliaetus

You teach us that we cannot stop trying to say something
even when the stilled world is not listening.

When all other voices have fallen silent, you rave on,
keeping the faith in the power of a few well-chosen syllables.

'Tok, tok, tok,' your spirit-tongue resounds off the roof of the world.

What vanity! What cheek! Your black, monkish figure trails
across the frozen wastes in an incantatory trance.

Hairs bristling on your Roman nose,
you survey our little dramas, looking

for some trouble to startle us into action,
to move the story forward—

You hatch the word, an original mischief.

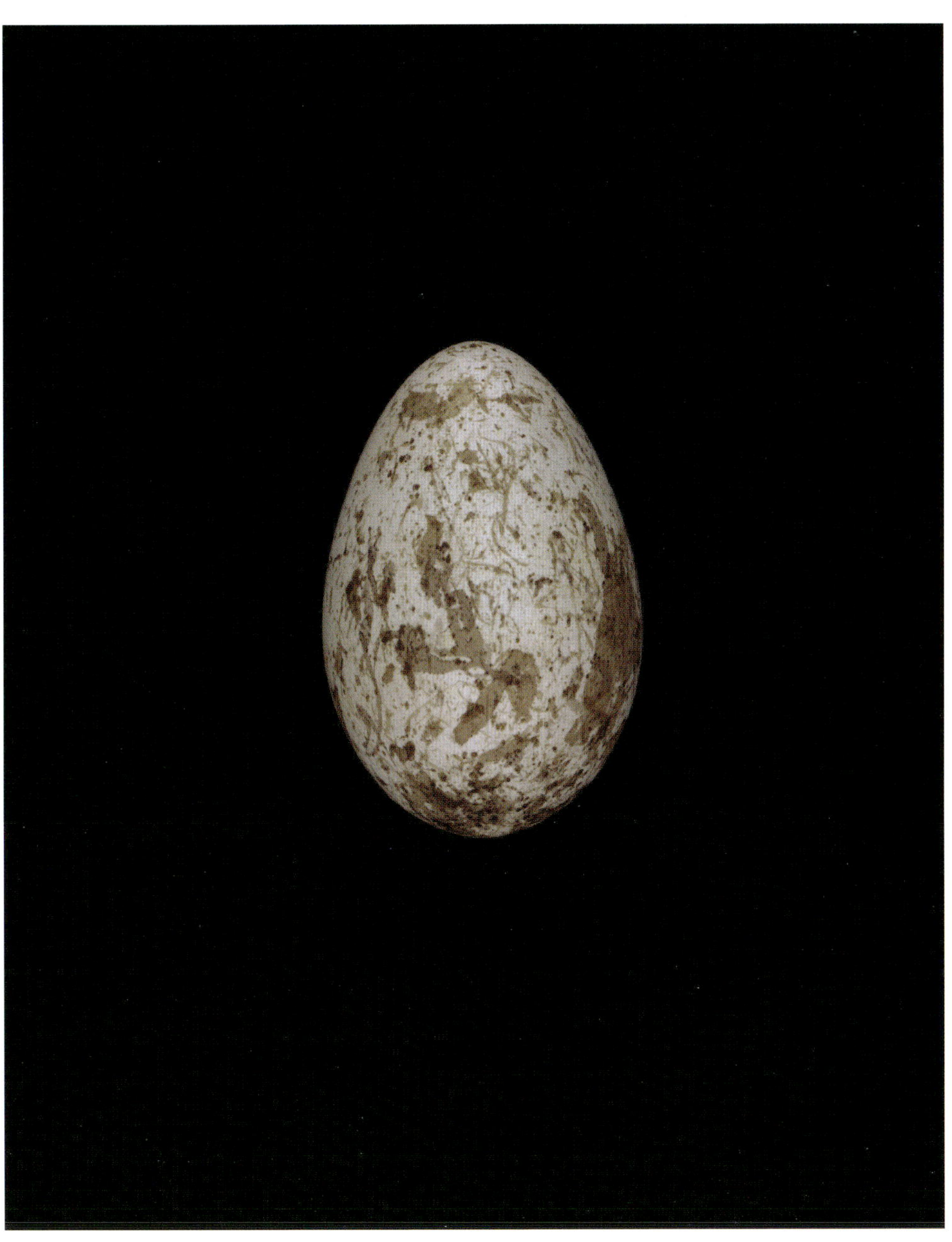

NORTHERN RAVEN
Corvus corax

The scarlet slash on the shoulder, bold epaulet,
reminds me of that dashing cad, Sergeant Troy,

whose sabre's lethal cuts and thrusts
opened the fickle heart of Bathsheba,

Hardy's 'Queen of the Corn-Market.'
The old master preferred the commonplace,

country-born, to the flash of rank or station.
Nature, too, favors the homely,

clothing the female in a drab cloak
that hides her well among the rushes.

She is the heroine; all that matters, her fate.
The dark, flashy one may mate as he likes

or explode in a hawk's talons, his red and black
feathers cascading down like fireworks.

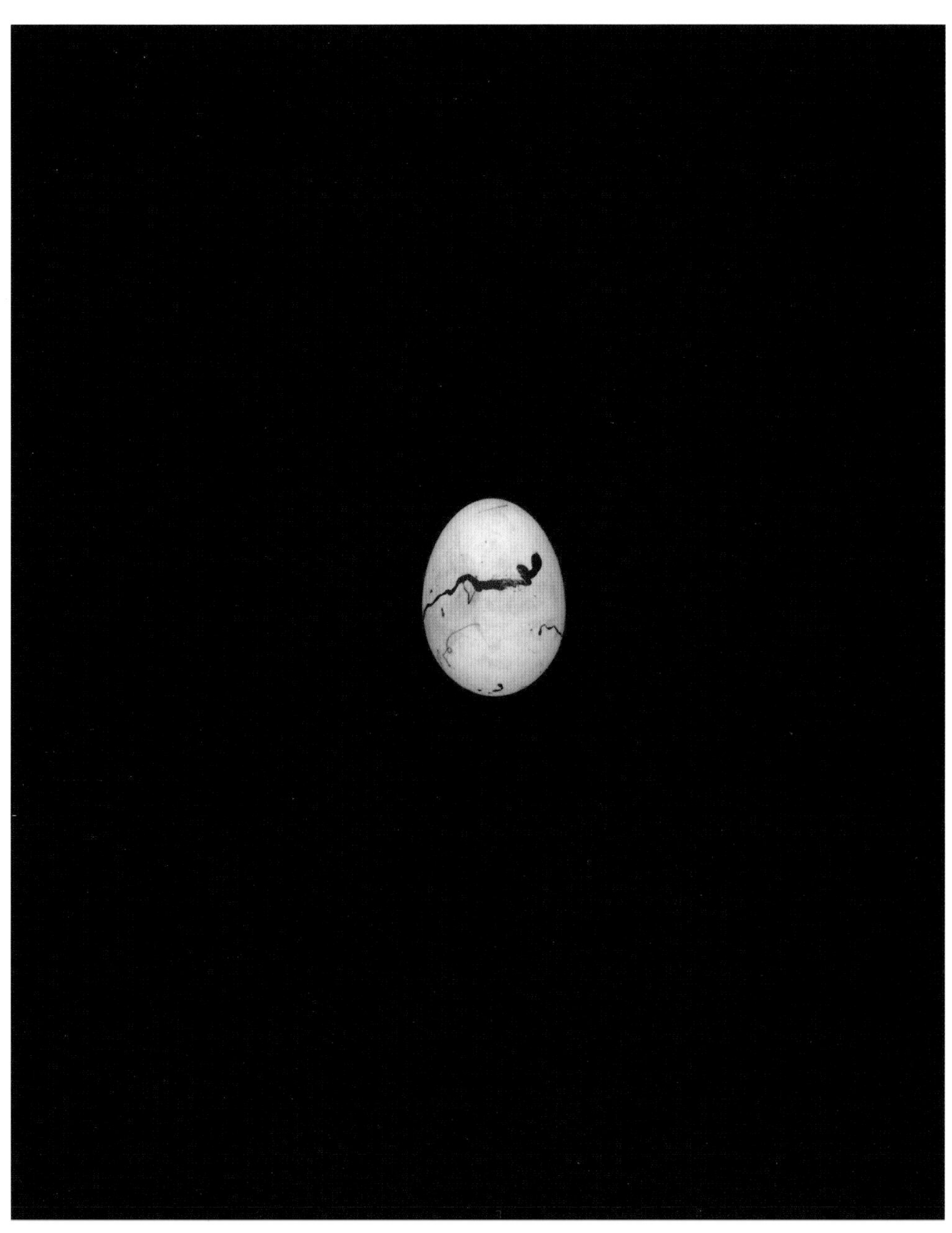

RED-WINGED BLACKBIRD
Agelaius phoeniceus

This egg creaks open like a hinge of rotten iron, mouth
bloodied by its gluttony of oxygen. Inside, ill omen.

Black birds burst from sour soil, strut over barren domain,
freezing all protest with opulent eyes.

They perch in rows, a dark battalion, uniformed,
weighing down the wires, our very speech.

Integers on an abacus, they ask the same question, over
and over, until our heads implode for want of a solution.

When they cloud the sky above the dying earth,
we withdraw into the dank recesses of resignation:

The time is come, there is no turning back.

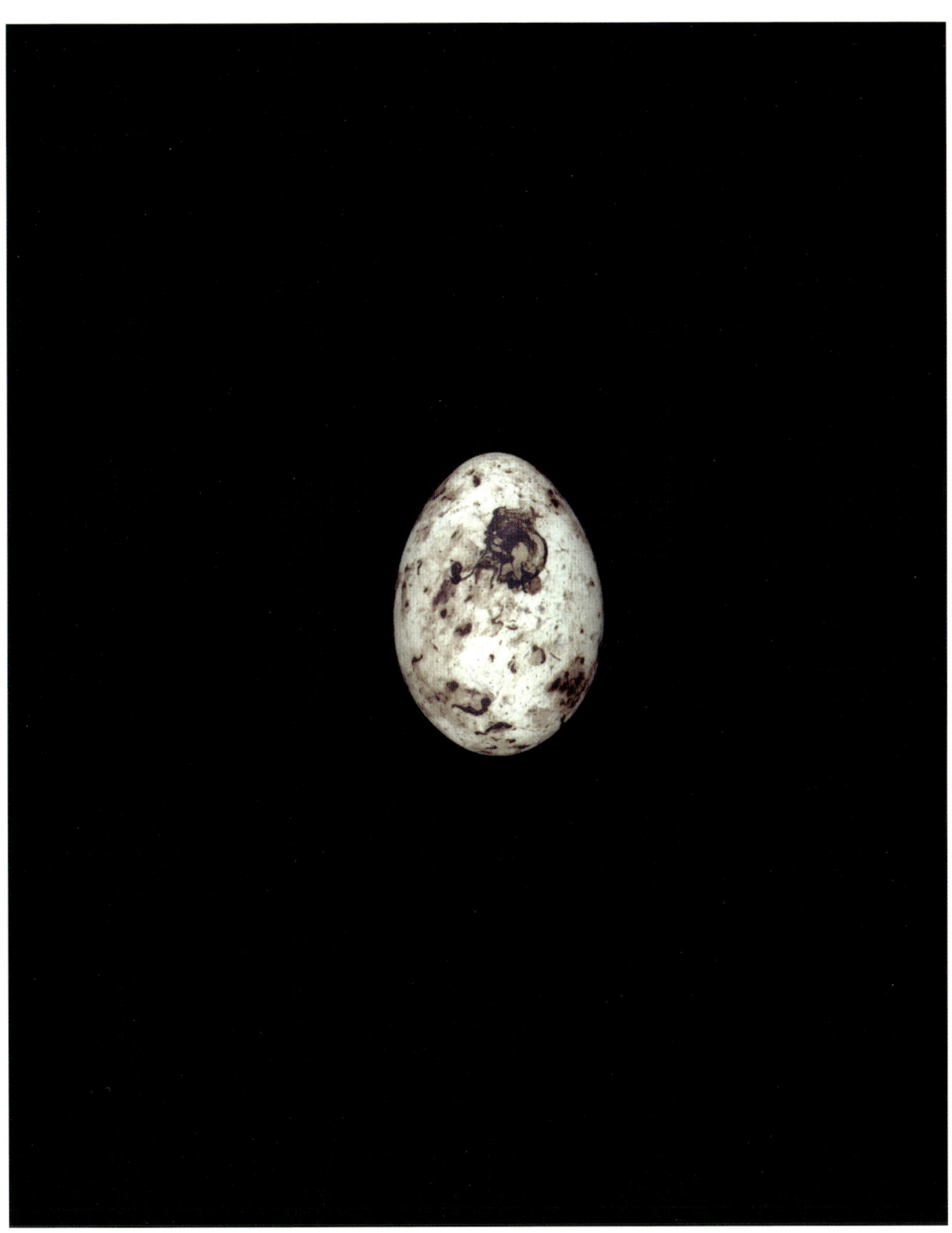

COMMON GRACKLE
Quiscalus quiscula

So birds must fly?
To that, I, emu, put the lie.

Down under, the world on its head,
birds walk instead.

True, females lay eggs, as everywhere,
but it is the males who take care

of the clutch of seven to ten.
The striped young soon run

with their faithful parents, like dinosaurs
kicking along at 50 kilometres an hour,

in a race to outdistance time.
I, emu, am the last of my kind.

EMU
Dromaius novaehollandiae

THE EGGS REPRESENTED IN 'OVA AVES' ARE FROM
THE BIOLOGY DEPARTMENT COLLECTION, MOUNT ALLISON UNIVERSITY,
SACKVILLE, NEW BRUNSWICK. THE ORIGINAL PHOTOGRAPHS ARE CHROMOGENIC
PRINTS MADE FROM 4 X 5 NEGATIVES. DESIGN BY ROBERT TOMBS, OTTAWA.
PRINTED BY PROPRINT SERVICES INC., TORONTO. PUBLISHED 2011
BY THE ANCHORAGE PRESS, JOLICURE, NEW BRUNSWICK.
WWW.ANCHORAGEPRESS.CA; WWW.HOLOWNIA.COM
THIS IS AN EDITION OF 1500
ISBN 978-1-895488-45-6